Bridge

for people who don't
know one card from another

Bridge

for people who don't
know one card from another

Ray Young
updated and edited by Sally Brock
Bridge Columnist of **The Sunday Times**

foulsham
LONDON • NEW YORK • TORONTO • SYDNEY

foulsham

The Publishing House, Bennetts Close, Cippenham, Slough, Berkshire, SL1 5AP, England

Foulsham books can be found in all good bookshops and direct from www.foulsham.com

ISBN: 978-0-572-03301-9

Playing cards used with permission from Ravensburger Ltd

Cover photograph © Superstock

A CIP record for this book is available from the British Library

The moral right of the author has been asserted

Printed in Dubai

Contents

Preface

Countless thousands of bright youngsters (and oldsters) deny themselves the pleasures of Contract Bridge because they think they'll appear stupid at their first lesson. Other countless thousands never get past the first page of even a basic beginners' Bridge book.

Bridge is not that hard once you leap the first hurdles, but the first hurdles can seem imposing indeed to someone who has never played a card game more complicated than Snap. The fact that there are 52 cards to keep track of seems like just too much. Complicate this further with suits and no-trumps, doubles and redoubles, and a bewildering jargon understandable only to the initiates, and the average beginner needs the courage of a lion to sit down at the Bridge table!

This book strips aside the mystery that baffles beginners. It explains all the basics that you need to know before you can play, or even read about, the game intelligently.

For best results, try to read this book all the way through in one sitting. In an hour or so you will have a good picture of what the game of Contract Bridge is all about. Then go back at your leisure and study each section. In less time and with less effort than you ever thought possible, you'll be playing Bridge, the *best* of all card games.

Throughout the book, players are referred to as 'he' rather than constantly and annoyingly repeating 'he or she', which does nothing to enhance the easy and clear communication that is the essence of this book.

One Card from Another

Bridge is a card game played by four people who may sometimes shout at each other but still manage to have a lot of fun. Two are partners against the other two.

Partners sit facing each other, ideally at a smallish (about 1m/3ft) square table. This is a handy arrangement if they get cross; they can glare and holler and mutter, but the table between them keeps them from exchanging blows!

The game is played with two packs of cards, though only one pack is used at a time. There are fifty-two cards in each pack after you throw out the jokers and Bridge scoring table (on second thoughts, keep that: it might come in handy later) that come with each new pack. The pack contains four **suits** of thirteen cards each: spades, hearts, diamonds and clubs. The three cards in each suit are, in ascending order, the 2 (sometimes known as the deuce), 3, 4, 5, 6, 7, 8, 9, 10, jack (or knave), queen, king and ace (though there are other card games in which the ace is the lowest card). The five top cards (ace, king, queen, jack and 10) are known as **honour** cards.

Suits and Ranks

The most important suit – the one that has the highest **rank** – is spades. The word spades comes from the Spanish word espadas, meaning swords, carried only by noblemen. As you will learn later, spades can be a very noble suit indeed.

The next most important suit is hearts. This suit designation originated in France in the 16th century and is named after the shape of its symbol. You'll find later that you can make beautiful music with cards of this suit — if you have enough of them.

The next most important suit is diamonds. And this suit got its name not from diamonds but from tiles. Somebody, way back when, tilted a tile on its side and decided it looked very much like a diamond.

The least important, lowest-ranking suit of all is clubs. How this suit got its name is a mystery. The symbol for clubs is really a cloverleaf.

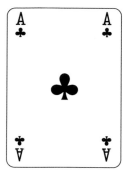

Spades and hearts are known as the **major** suits, while diamonds and clubs are the **minors**.

Dealing the Cards

Before you start the game, take one pack and **cut** for partners. Each player in turn picks up a good proportion of the pack (say between five and fifteen cards) and reveals the bottom card. The player who cuts the highest card chooses where to sit and which of two packs of cards to start playing with and also becomes **dealer**. If two are the same number, then the winner is the one of higher rank. The player who cuts the next highest card sits opposite him and becomes his partner. The others take the remaining two seats.

The dealer then shuffles the pack well (seven **riffle-shuffles** are recommended) and passes it to the player on his right for him to cut. Cut in this context means to take a fair proportion of cards, say between ten and forty, from the top of the pack, and then to put the top portion on the bottom. The purpose of this is to prevent any sharp dealer giving himself a good hand.

While this is going on, the dealer's partner shuffles the other pack and places it on his right, ready for the next deal, which will be made by the player on the dealer's left.

The dealer distributes all fifty-two cards, face down, one at a time to each player in a clockwise direction. The first person to get a card is the player to the left of the dealer. The last one to get a card is the dealer, and if the dealer has done a good job without being fumble-fingered, each person finishes up with thirteen cards. Your thirteen cards make up your **hand**.

Sorting your Hand

Unless you have the memory, cunning and expert card sense of a riverboat gambler, you will want to sort your thirteen cards into some kind of order. This sorting isn't hard to do at all.

Put all your cards in each suit together. You will find it easier to select your cards if you sort your suits in a red-black-red-black order, though this isn't strictly necessary. Now put all your cards in each suit in ascending order, working from right to left.

What is a Trick?

The concept of a **trick** occurs in many games. Each player, in clockwise order, contributes one card, and these cards form a trick. In Bridge, because each player starts with thirteen cards, there are thirteen tricks in each game.

When a particular suit is led to a trick, the other players must play a card of the same suit if they have one.

What is a Trump?

The word **trump** comes from a fine old Latin word triumphus, and a trump card can, indeed, triumph. One of the four suits is selected as trumps and that suit automatically ranks higher than any card in any other suit in the pack. Many games other than Bridge use trumps and the suit that is to be trumps can be selected in a number of different ways. Sometimes the dealer cuts the pack to select trumps, but in Bridge the players decide by means of the **bidding**, or **auction** (see page 43).

In Bridge, it is also possible to play without trumps, i.e. in **no-trumps**. No-trumps outranks all the four suits.

How to Win a Trick in No-trumps

Let's look at a sample no-trump trick.

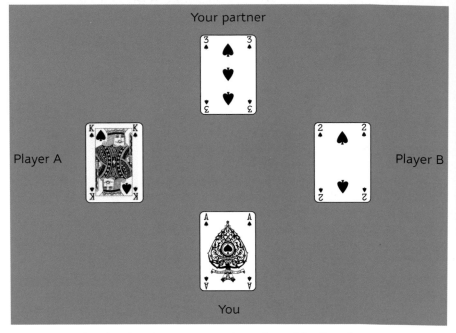

Player A **leads**, that is, puts a card on the table first (how that is decided will come later), followed by your partner, Player B, then you. The trick is simply won by the highest ranking card played in the suit led. In this example, you win the trick because you have the highest card, the ace.

How to Win a Trick in a Suit Contract

In a **suit contract** tricks can be won even by low cards *if* they are in the trump suit and *if* you don't have any cards in the suit led.

Your partner

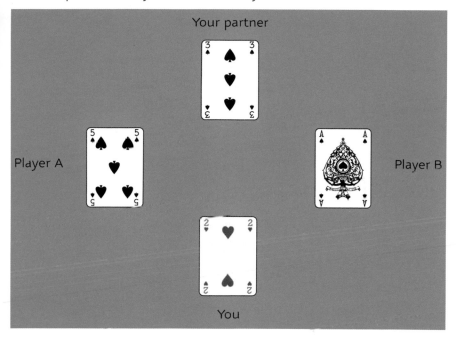

Player A

Player B

You

In this example, hearts are trumps. Again, Player A leads to this trick. Your partner and Player B both **follow suit**, but you have no spades: you are **void** in that suit.

You can choose to win the trick with a small trump (the 2 of hearts). However, it is not compulsory to play a trump. You could play a card in a different suit instead. That card is called a **discard**. In that case Player B would have won the trick because he played the highest spade.

Your 2 of hearts won the trick from the ace of spades; you didn't have any spades but you did have hearts and hearts were trumps. You **ruffed** (or trumped) Player B's ace of spades.

Bridge is a Partnership Game

Because Bridge is a partnership game, it doesn't matter which player of that partnership wins any trick. If your partner plays the king of a suit to a particular trick, generally speaking you would not play your ace to beat him. The game is about co-operation.

If you read Bridge articles in newspapers (something that is highly recommended), you will see that those partnerships are usually referred to as North/South and East/West, and they appear in diagrams laid out in the way you would expect, with South at the bottom, North at the top, West on the left and East on the right. That is what we will use from now on.

MiniBridge

In Bridge, there are two main elements: the bidding and the play. Since the bidding happens first and decides the final **contract** (i.e. who is trying to make how many tricks with what trumps, if any), the bidding is usually taught before the play. However, this can mean that it is a long while before a beginner gets to play the cards and it can become boring. One of the greatest innovations in the teaching of Bridge in recent years has been the development of **MiniBridge**. This is a way of putting the bidding aside for a while.

The quickest and easiest way to tell whether or not you have a good hand – a hand that will win tricks – is to use the point-count system. This is just a simple way of assigning values to the cards you have in your hand and it is used in MiniBridge and Bridge.

After you have dealt and sorted your cards, the first thing to do is to count your **high-card points**:

- Ace: 4 points
- King: 3 points
- Queen: 2 points
- Jack: 1 point.

Each player adds up his points and announces the total in turn, starting with the dealer.

The partnership with the higher total will become the **declaring side**, and the other partnership is the **defending side**. If they both have 20 points, deal again. Of the declaring side, the player with the higher points total will become **declarer**, while his partner is the **dummy**. If they have the same, the first to announce becomes declarer.

Here is an example deal. It will help you to follow the play if you deal out a pack of cards and play it through.

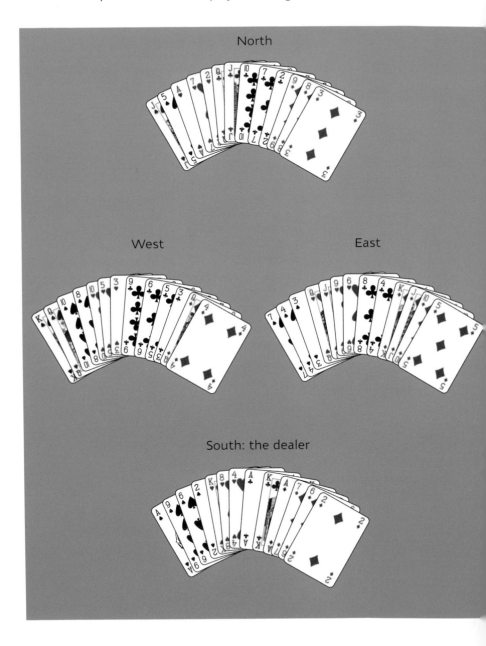

North

West   East

South: the dealer

South, the dealer, starts by announcing: 'I have 18 points.' Then West: '7 points', North: '8 points', and East: '7 points'. So North/South's total is 26 points, while East/West have only 14. So North/South is the declaring side, and South is the declarer.

The next thing to happen is that North puts all his thirteen cards down on the table, arranged like this:

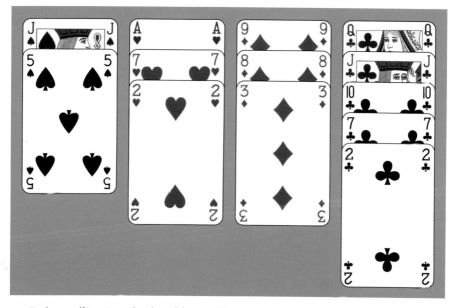

To be polite, South should say, 'Thank you, partner.' North becomes the dummy and plays no further part in the proceedings – though you can always send him off to make the tea!

South now has to decide what are trumps, if indeed there should be any. As a guideline to get you started you should choose to play with a trump suit if you have eight or more cards in a suit between your two hands, otherwise settle for no-trumps. So, here South should choose to play without trumps, i.e. in no-trumps.

Later (see page 24) we will discuss using targets to decide how many tricks South should aim to make, but to start with both sides should just attempt to make as many tricks as possible.

The player to the left of declarer, here West, starts by making an **opening lead**. Against no-trumps you should generally lead your longest suit; and with two suits of equal length you should generally choose your strongest. Here the king of spades stands out. West places that card in the middle of the table.

South now needs to play a card from the dummy, either reaching forward to play the card himself, or else calling for a card for dummy to play for him: '5 of spades, please, partner', or 'Small, please, partner.' That card should also be played in the middle of the table, near to West's card but not obscuring it. East would play the 3 of spades and South the ace, also in the middle of the table.

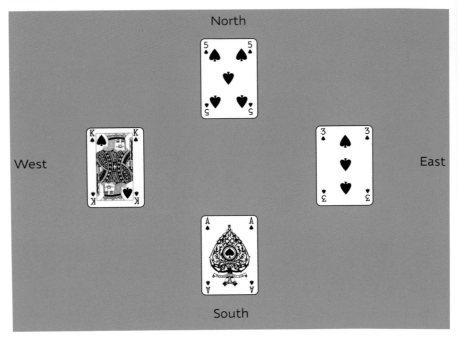

South has won the trick and should gather the cards together into a neat stack and place the trick face down in front of him. The tricks should be stacked in a neat overlapping pile at the edge of the table so that it is easy to see how many tricks North/South have won.

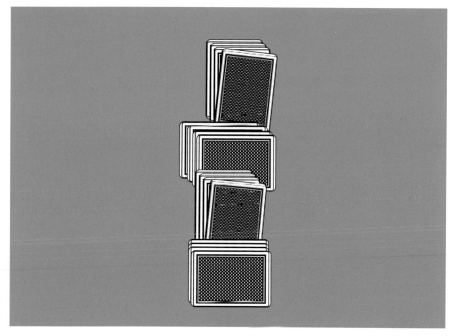

Because South won trick one, he is the one to lead to trick two. At this point (or, better, before he plays from dummy at all) South should pause to consider how many more tricks he is likely to win. This is likely to be one spade, two hearts, one diamond and five club tricks – nine in all. However, he has to be a little careful about the order in which he takes them. Suppose he starts by playing the ace and king of hearts, followed by the ace of diamonds and the ace and king of clubs. Now, although dummy has three club winners (queen, jack, 10), declarer has no way of reaching them because he has no clubs left in his own hand, so he will make only six tricks.

The correct first move is to play (or **cash**) the ace and king of clubs. Then play a heart to dummy's ace and take the other three club tricks. The king of hearts and ace of diamonds in hand bring the total up to nine.

Let's look at another example:

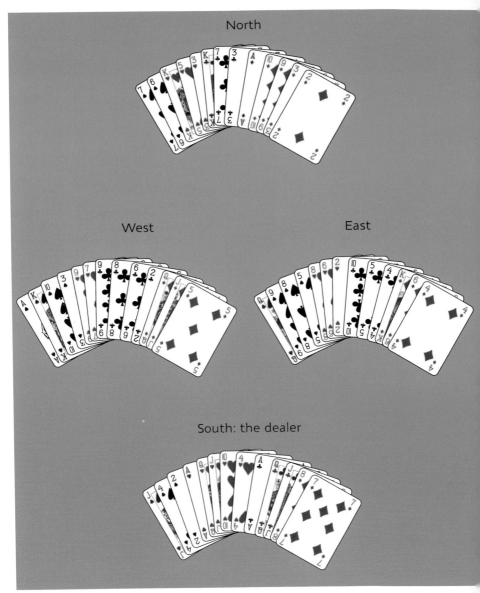

Again, the points are announced: South, 15 points; West, 10 points; North, 10 points; and East, 5 points. This time North/South's total is 25 points, while East/West have 15. Again, North/South is the declaring side and South is the declarer.

After North has put dummy down on the table, South has to decide what trumps are, if indeed there should be any. Here, with eight hearts between the two hands, South should choose hearts as trumps.

When South has chosen trumps, dummy should move that suit so that it is on the left (from declarer's viewpoint).

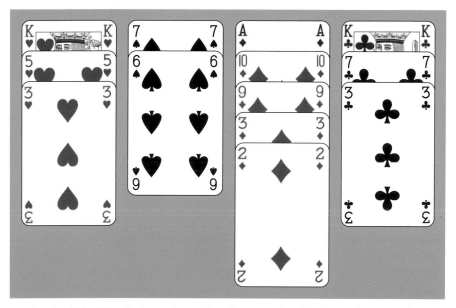

Again, it is West's turn to make the opening lead. Against a suit contract, a good choice is a suit where you have two touching honour cards, so the ace of spades stands out. As there is no honour card to beat an ace and none of the other players is void in spades, the ace of spades wins the trick.

Because West has won the trick, East should gather the trick and place it face down in front of him, allowing West to get on with the serious business of leading to the next trick. Whether East or West now win any more tricks, East is the trick-gatherer for the partnership.

West continues with the king of spades, and again the other three players follow with smaller spades, so West also wins trick two.

Now that dummy is out of spades and will be able to ruff the next spade, West changes tack and plays a club, hoping that East can win a trick there. However, South wins trick three with the jack of clubs, and gathers that trick and places it on the table in front of him.

South should now count his tricks (again, it would have been better to stop and do that before playing any card at all): five hearts, one diamond and three clubs, making nine in total. Maybe, because it is only his second deal, South should settle for that; but can you see a way to make an extra trick?

South can make an extra trick by ruffing a spade in the North hand. The first thing to do is cash the ace of hearts, just to make sure that neither opponent has all five outstanding trumps. Then South plays the jack of spades from hand and ruffs it with dummy's king of hearts. This is followed by the 5 of hearts from dummy and the queen from South's hand, then the rest of the trumps, two remaining club winners and the ace of diamonds.

Setting Targets

When you have played a few deals of MiniBridge you will find that you want to set targets. Simply trying to make as many tricks as possible is not very challenging. Besides, it is only fitting that the more high-card points you hold, the more tricks you should try to make. Here is a sensible schedule:

Points	Number of tricks
21–22	Seven
23–24	Eight
25–26	Nine
27–28	Ten
29–32	Eleven
33–36	Twelve
37+	Thirteen

You will notice very quickly that these targets are much easier to fulfil when you have a *good fit*, that is, a lot of trumps between your two hands, or in no-trumps when you have a **long suit**. When you come to play Bridge you will discover that you should let the degree of fit influence your bidding just as much as high-card points.

On the deals we played through earlier, North/South had 25 or 26 points so their target would have been nine tricks. On the first, careful play by South would see him fulfilling his contract. On the second, if he remembered to ruff the spade in the dummy the target would have been exceeded by one trick – he would have scored an **overtrick**.

Your Play

The play described in this chapter applies equally to Bridge and MiniBridge. If you aren't certain that you know the order of the cards, the rank of the suits and how tricks are won in trump and no-trump contracts, go back and read the pages 9–24 again.

You must understand these basic principles clearly. Once you do, you'll be able to pluck a card out of your hand and plonk it on the table with confidence. Otherwise, you'll just sit there fumbling and annoying the living daylights out of everybody else in the game.

Playing the cards involves one of two things: **offence** or **defence**. On offence you are trying to make enough tricks to bring home your contract; you are declarer. In defence, you are trying to win enough tricks to **set** or defeat your opponents' contract; you are a **defender**.

Offence

Planning Your Play

In Bridge, he who hesitates is *not* lost, providing that he hesitates at the right time. The right time is the instant your partner spreads his hand as dummy. Study his hand and then yours. See how they fit. Count the tricks you are most likely to lose. Then figure ways to avoid losing these tricks.

Don't be afraid to take your time before playing to trick one, even if your play is obvious. Some players have an irritating habit of playing for you when there is a **singleton** in dummy. Then the next defender might perhaps play, too. You may feel foolish for having a think, but don't let them rush you. This is the time to think about the whole hand, not just the first trick.

The Finesse

One of your most useful weapons on offence is the **finesse** because it's one of the few ways a smaller card can steal a trick from a bigger card. This tricky manoeuvre is best explained by an example:

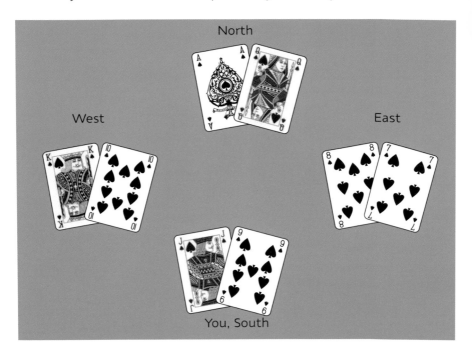

Your partner's queen is lower in rank than West's king, but it can steal a trick – quite legitimately, of course. Simply lead to your partner's hand by playing the 9 of spades; then if the left-hand opponent plays the 10, you play the queen. Voilà! You have successfully finessed the king of spades and won a trick with a smaller card, namely your queen of spades. Of course, if West had played the king of spades you would have won with your ace, and then your queen would have scored a trick on the next round.

Alternatively, the layout might be:

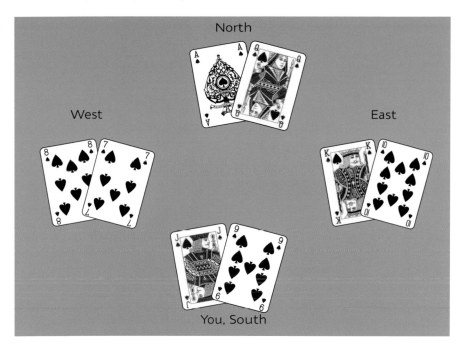

North

West

East

You, South

Now your queen of spades will lose to East's king, but in that case you would have lost a trick whatever you did. A finesse works exactly half the time.

Incidentally, there are lots of finesses you can try, as you will learn after playing for a while, but bear in mind that a finesse gives you only a 50:50 chance of success. You should always plan your play to get better odds if you possibly can.

Playing in a No-trump Contract

Planning your play in a no-trump contract is straightforward. You don't have to worry about the opponents ruffing your winners. All you have to worry about is having enough winners.

First, count your winners in **high cards**: your aces, kings, queens, etc. If your total doesn't quite come up to the number of tricks you need for your contract, even with a successful finesse or two, look for a suit that can bring you in winners with **long cards**. Maybe you can afford to lose two tricks out of five in a suit. The two tricks you give up might produce three winners in long cards: not a bad trade. Simply look for a five-card suit in your hand or dummy's, and start losing the tricks you must lose right away.

A word of caution about no-trumps, however: no-trump contracts are about one trick harder to play than trump contracts, so don't bid no-trumps willy-nilly. You might regret not having a few trumps to take care of the opponents' high cards.

Playing in a Suit Contract

Here are a few of the ways to avoid losers in a suit contract:

- You can take a finesse in trumps or any other suit.
- You can play out your aces and kings, hoping to **drop** a missing honour such as a queen. This is a slightly superior play to a finesse when you and your partner hold nine cards in a suit that is missing the queen.
- You can ruff losers. A void, singleton or **doubleton** in dummy in a side suit is pure gold if dummy has enough trumps. Before touching trumps, play on the suit in which dummy is short. When dummy has no card left in that suit you can use dummy's trumps to ruff your losers.
- You can discard losers. For instance, if you have ace-king of a suit in dummy and no cards of that suit in your hand, you can discard two of your hand's losers on the good ace-king. To make sure you have a good ace-king, you'd better extract the opponents' trumps first, i.e. **draw** trumps. It's always a pity to see a noble king get pounced on by a lonely 2 of trumps. Sometimes, however, you have to take the gamble that your good tricks might be trumped. You try for quick discards and hope for the best.
- You can use your trumps to help you set up winners in your long suit. By ruffing your opponents' winners in your long suit, you will eventually set up the small cards.

There is one more decision you'll have to make while you're pausing to plan your play: should you draw the opponents' trumps right away or not?

Dummy holds:

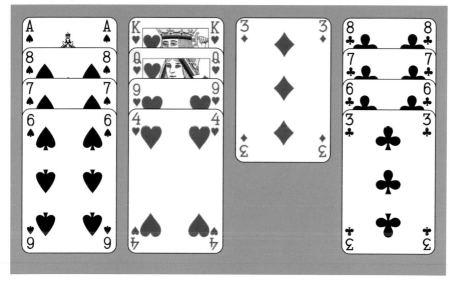

You hold:

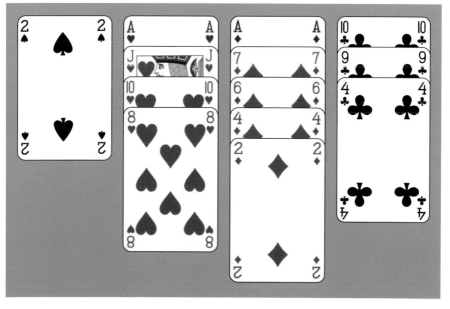

If you're forced to play trumps four times to extract them from the opponents, your hand (including your partner's hand) will collapse in a heap of losers. What do you do? Your opponents will probably lead clubs, which will ensure your losing the first three tricks. On the fourth trick, however, you take command no matter whether the defenders now play a spade or a diamond. You cash the ace of diamonds and the ace of spades and then proceed to ruff spades in your own hand and diamonds in the dummy, making all eight of your trumps. Even if one of your opponents holds the remaining five trump cards it will make no difference, because your trumps are all higher. Add your ace of spades and your ace of diamonds to your eight trump tricks and you arrive at a total of ten tricks, way ahead of your MiniBridge target (actually, since you have fewer than 20 points between you, you would have been the defending side at MiniBridge) and enough for **game** at Bridge (see page 41).

Notice, though, that had one of your opponents played a trump after taking the first three tricks your possible trump tricks would have been reduced to seven.

This way of playing a hand, whereby you get the most possible mileage out of your trumps by ruffing back and forth from dummy's hand to yours, is known as a **cross-ruff**. It's a possible line of play you should always be on the alert for, especially when it looks as if you have more losers than you can handle.

Defence

Your Opening Lead

A staggering number of contracts are won or lost on the opening lead. Finding the right opening lead is a combination of science, art and intuition. MiniBridge is easier than Bridge in that you get to see the dummy before you make your opening lead, but in Bridge you often know more about partner's distribution and likely high-card location. Here are some guidelines that apply to MiniBridge and Bridge.

- **Lead from an honour sequence.** If you have a sequence of touching honours, such as queen, jack, 10 or king, queen, jack, lead the top of the sequence, i.e. the queen or king respectively.

- **Lead through dummy's suit.** There might be a broken suit such as ace, queen, 10, 9. You might be able to establish the king, and maybe the jack too, as tricks for your partner.

- **Lead a trump.** You may bust up a beautiful cross-ruff or cut down the ruffing power of the dummy. This is an especially good idea when dummy has a singleton or void in a side suit.

- **Lead a singleton or a doubleton.** This is a particularly good lead if you have a short but potent trump holding such as king, 9, 2, and you know your partner has quite a few points. If he has an ace or a king (i.e. an **entry**), you may be able to use it to reach his hand so that he can return the suit your singleton was in, and you can score one of your little trumps by ruffing.

- **Lead a long suit and force declarer.** If you have a good collection of trump cards (four or more), it's often a good idea to lead a suit you think the declarer may have to ruff. If you keep leading this suit at every opportunity, you may wind up with more trumps than the declarer – and this is an embarrassing and costly predicament for him.

- **Lead your longest and strongest suit.** Defending against a no-trump contract, your idea is to win as many long-card tricks as you can in addition to your high-card tricks. It is generally best to lead a five-card suit against a no-trump contract, however weak it is. Suppose you hold:

Lead a heart against a no-trump contract. If you try a top diamond first, that might give up an entry you need for setting up the hearts. Against a suit contract it is different and you should start with a top diamond.

There is a **convention** when leading a long suit to lead your fourth highest card, i.e. the fourth from the top. From king, 9, 6, 2, lead the 2; from king, 9, 7, 6, 2, lead the 6. Your partner can often work out from the lead how many you have and therefore how to defend.

The only times you *don't* lead fourth best are:

- When you have a long sequence of touching honours (ace, king, queen, 3); or

- When you have an **interior sequence** (king, jack, 10, 8, 3), lead the jack in hope of knocking out one of the opponents' high cards in a hurry.

Some General Principles of Defence

The first thing you must do when defending is to figure out exactly how many tricks you need in order to set the contract. This will depend on the target.

Total up your rock-solid certain tricks, your highly probable tricks, and then plan your defence just as carefully as you would plan the play of one of your own contracts. Be prepared to change your plan as the play progresses and you gather more evidence concerning what your partner and the declarer hold.

Defence is the toughest part of Bridge. It calls for more calculation and more alertness than any other phase of the game. Here are a few guidelines, but remember: each must be tempered with common sense and even ignored at times; vigilance and experience will tell you when.

- **Second hand low.** When you are second to play to a trick, it rarely pays to squander your high cards by playing them on opponents' low cards. Play a waiting game. Maybe your partner can take the trick more cheaply. In a finesse situation, your opponent might chicken out and not take the finesse. High cards are best used to overtake other high cards. Don't waste them on 2s and 3s unless you have an urgent reason to take a trick. This might be to get in quickly in order to return your partner's first-led suit if you suspect it was a singleton and you can now give him a ruff.

- **Third hand high.** When you are third to play to a trick, play as high as you need to take the trick or force out a high card from the fourth hand. This doesn't mean you automatically play your highest card. Sometimes your next highest card will do the job you want it to as in this case:

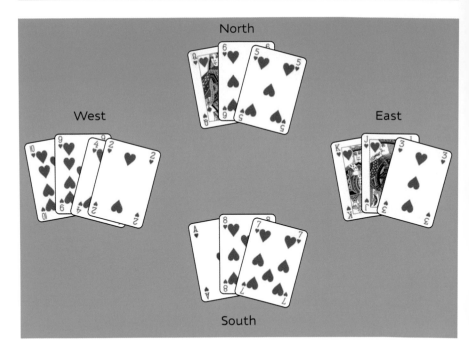

North

West

East

South

Partner leads the 2 of hearts, dummy plays low and you should play the jack – not the king. The jack will force out South's ace quite nicely; hang on to your king and it will be in perfect position to capture the queen next time your partner leads.

- **Play through strength.** When the dummy is on your left, it usually pays to lead through a strong but slightly fractured suit, such as ace, queen, 10 or king, jack, 9. However, if the suit is long, beware, because you may be doing the opponents' work for them and setting up long tricks for discards.

- **Play up to weakness.** 'When the dummy's on your right, lead the weakest suit in sight' is a sage-old motto. If dummy has small cards, declarer has to play a high card in an attempt to win the trick and all your partner need do is beat declarer's card.

- **Cover an honour with an honour.** When declarer leads an honour from his hand and dummy has a higher honour, you should **cover** declarer's honour with your honour. For example:

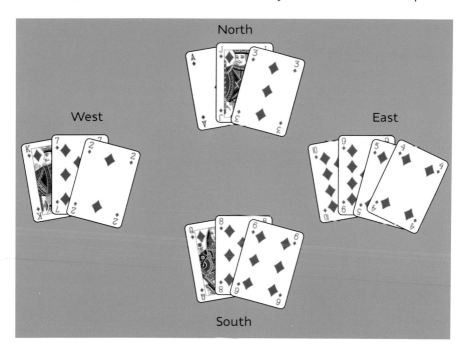

North

West

East

South

If declarer plays the queen of diamonds from hand and you play low, the queen will win the trick. A later finesse of your king will give declarer three diamond tricks. If you cover the queen of diamonds with the king, declarer can never make more than two tricks.

- **Return your partner's suit.** When your partner has made the opening lead, give him credit for having led the suit he did. He may have had a singleton or doubleton, or an honour that he led away from. Unless you're in a great rush to carry out some fiendish plan of your own, it's generally a good idea to return a card in partner's suit. Opening up some other suit for no good reason is likely to help declarer.

- **Signal high-low.** When your partner leads an honour and you want to encourage him to continue the suit, play a high card. When discarding, play a high card if you want partner to play that suit. When declarer is leading a suit, play high-low to show an even number. This can help partner know how to defend.

Remember these general principles on offence and defence are not engraved on tablets of stone, but some direction is better than none. Use these principles when you have nothing better to guide you, and your game will at least be adequate; for a beginner, it will be astonishingly good.

How Bidding Works

Bidding is a different, more complex way of arriving at a contract, than the simple point-count method used in MiniBridge. It allows a much greater use of judgement in working out whether or not the hands fit well.

You bid at the start of the game, each player taking it in turns to make a bid, starting with the dealer. Bidding always goes clockwise. Bidding stops when three people in a row pass (except on the first round when all four need to pass before the deal is thrown in, i.e. redealt by the same player). The last bid before the three passes becomes the final contract, setting the target and the trump suit, if any. Then the play starts.

Making a Bid

A **bid** is composed of two parts: a number and a **denomination**. For example, two hearts or four no-trumps. You do not have to make a bid; you can **pass** or, if an opponent has bid, **double** instead.

Since there are thirteen tricks in a game of Bridge, the average number for one side to make in any denomination would be six and a half. So, those six tricks (dispensing of the half) are more or less a given. In order for a hand to be in any way special it has to contract for more than an average number of tricks. Hence, to bid two hearts means that a player is suggesting that his partnership will make six plus two tricks with hearts as trumps, i.e. eight tricks. Similarly, four no-trumps means ten tricks without trumps.

As there are 40 high-card points in the pack, the average is 10 and you would not consider making an **opening bid** with fewer than 10 high-card points.

The dealer gets the first chance to bid. If his hand looks as if it wouldn't take very many tricks without a lot of help from partner, he can say 'Pass', perhaps with a hand something like this:

Then the player on his left gets a chance to bid. Perhaps he has a better hand and can make a bid. The lowest bid he can make is one club, contracting for seven tricks with clubs as trumps. This would be a possible hand:

The highest bid anyone can make is seven no-trumps, which would probably make everybody else at the table keel over in a dead faint. For example:

This type of hand is so strong, though, that you would be unlikely ever to hold it.

Since any new bid must outrank the last bid, the rank of the suits becomes very important.

An Example Auction

Here's an example bidding sequence to show how it works.

- You deal and bid one club, your opening bid.

- The next player on your left bids one heart. This bid by the side which did not open is called an **overcall**.

- Your partner bids two diamonds. Because diamonds are lower-ranking than hearts, they cannot be bid without raising the level of the auction.

- The player to his left (on your right) bids two spades.

- You bid two no-trumps, which outranks all suits.

- The next player passes with nothing more to say.

- Your partner bids three no-trumps.

- The other three players pass, so the contract is three no-trumps. Your side has bought the contract and becomes the **declaring side**. In Bridge it is the player who first bids the denomination the contract winds up in who plays the hand with his partner as dummy. You were the first player to bid no-trumps so you must try to make nine tricks without trumps.

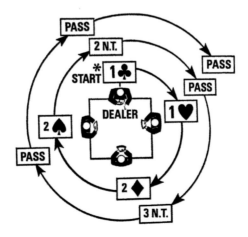

The Game Bonus

You may wonder why, in the foregoing auction, your partner bid three no-trumps. There was no need to do so in order to win the contract because you had made the previous bid of two no-trumps.

In MiniBridge we set targets according to how many points we held. In Bridge our target is to make game. Scoring in Bridge is described in some detail in Chapter 7 (see page 59), but it is impossible to proceed without some knowledge of it.

For every trick bid and made in excess of six, you score

- Minor suits (diamonds and clubs): 20 points

- Major suits (spades and hearts): 30 points

- No-trumps: 40 points for the first trick, 30 points for each subsequent trick.

You make game when you have scored a total of 100 points. These points are known as contract points and are scored **below the line** (see page 59). So game in a minor suit needs you to bid and make five clubs or five diamonds (making eleven tricks), game in a major needs you to bid and make four hearts or four spades (ten tricks), while game in no-trumps needs you to bid and make three no-trumps (nine tricks). Making game is very desirable, attracting a bonus of several hundred points (see page 60).

It is not necessary to do this in one go. Suppose on deal one you bid two hearts and make eight tricks. That gives you 60 points. If on deal two you bid two spades and make eight tricks, you have a total of 120 points and score your game bonus. However, should your opponents on deal two bid and make a game, three no-trumps, say, then your **partscore** of 60 points is neutralised; you still score those 60 points, but have to start again in terms of working towards a game bonus. Because of this there is a great premium on bidding game, which is why your partner **raised** your two no-trumps to three no-trumps on the previous auction.

After the Auction

In Bridge, unlike MiniBridge, the person on declarer's left must lead a card before the dummy comes down, with the trumps on the left, as in MiniBridge.

Bidding

Although we have already come across the concept of high-card points in the MiniBridge chapter, it may be useful to repeat it here.

High-card Points

The value of high-card points is fairly obvious: high cards outrank low cards. Aces and kings usually beat lesser cards and win more tricks.

- Ace: 4 points
- King: 3 points
- Queen: 2 points
- Jack: 1 point

Opening Bids

If you have 12 points you have enough to open the bidding. However, it is easier to make tricks when you have long suits than when your longest suit is only a four-carder. With ace, king, queen, jack, 3 of clubs, for instance, your three can take a trick *if* your higher cards can **strip** the opponents of all their clubs. (Remember: they *must* follow suit and play clubs if they have can.) Your 3 of clubs thereby becomes a long card and much of the time your 10 points will take five tricks. If you have ace, king, queen, jack alone, on the other hand, your 10 points would only ever make four tricks.

Consequently, open the bidding with 11 points if you have a good five-card suit; and with 10 points if you have a good six-card suit or two five-carders.

When we were playing MiniBridge, we said that if you had an eight-card fit between you, you should choose that suit as trumps, but with no eight-card fit you should choose no-trumps. In Bridge this is also a good general rule. However, because you need only nine tricks to make game in no-trumps or ten in a major, but need eleven to make game in a minor, it is more important to establish whether or not there is an eight-card (or better) fit in a major than in a minor. Most hands where the best fit is in a minor should be played in a partscore or no-trumps, because it is easier to make nine tricks for game in no-trumps than eleven tricks for game in a minor suit.

The first aim of bidding is to establish whether or not you have an eight-card major-suit fit.

Suit Contract Opening

You need a five-card suit to open one of a major. Otherwise open in a minor suit just to say that you have quite a good hand. Sometimes you might have to open in a three-card minor. Here are some examples of hands that are worth opening:

You have 13 high-card points and a five-card suit. Open one spade.

Here is an awkward hand. With no five-card major and a hand not strong enough to open one no-trump (see page 46), you have to open your **better minor**: one club.

Partner will now know that you have at least 12 points, but will not take your clubs too seriously. His first job is to discover if there is an eight-card major-suit fit.

No-trump Opening

To open the bidding with one no-trump, you need 15-17 points and a **balanced hand**, i.e. one with no singleton or void and no more than one doubleton. No-trump contracts are harder to play than trump contracts which is why you need more points to open one no-trump.

Here is a typical one no-trump opening:

A Big Hand

What if you have a *really* strong hand – a 'rock-crusher' – and it's your turn to open the bidding? Don't hide your light under a bushel; open two of something.

- Two no-trumps shows 20-22 points and a balanced hand.

- An opening bid of two diamonds, two hearts or two spades shows a very strong hand with a good suit of at least five cards. You should have at least 20 points or else eight and a half tricks in your own hand. With no support for the suit opened and no good suit of his own, your partner should respond two no-trumps.

- Two clubs is an artificial, conventional bid, having nothing to do with clubs. It simply shows either a balanced hand of 23-24 points, or any hand that can make game on its own, usually with about 25 points. Unless he has a good suit of his own, partner should respond two diamonds to give you room to describe your hand further.

Responding

An opening bid just starts things off nicely. You and your partner need about 25 or 26 points between you to make a game in hearts or spades (ten tricks) or no-trumps (nine tricks). For a game in clubs or diamonds (where you have to make eleven tricks), you and your partner should have about 29 points between you.

There are big bonuses for bidding and making a **slam**. A small slam is twelve tricks, and a grand slam all thirteen. For these you need a combined total of about 33 or 37 points respectively.

Once your partner opens the bidding with a suit, give him credit for at least 12 points and add your honour points to those (in your head, of course). If you have three-card support for a five-card major suit, you can count extra points for distribution (known as **distribution points**) as follows:

- A void: 3 points

- A singleton: 2 points

- A doubleton: 1 point.

If you have four-card support for a major, you can add a further 2 points.

As responder to the opening bid, if you have three or four cards in partner's major suit, raise that major with 5-9 points. If partner opens one heart, raise to two hearts. Then see what happens; it might be all the encouragement he needs to bid more. If you have 10-12 points make a **jump** raise to three hearts, asking him to go to game with anything more than a bare minimum hand. If you have more than that go directly to game (double jump raise to four hearts).

If you don't have support for partner you can bid a new suit (of at least four cards) at the one level with 6 or more points, but if it is lower ranking so you have to go to the two level then you need 10 points. These change-of-suit responses are **forcing**, i.e. partner must not pass. Because of this you can make the bids with a very strong hand, knowing that you will get another chance.

A one no-trump response shows 6-9 points with no fit for partner and no four-card major that could be bid at the one level. A two no-trump response shows 10-12 and three no-trumps 13-15, both with no fit for partner.

A jump bid in a new suit is forcing to game, showing 16 or more points and either a good suit of your own or a good fit for partner.

Rebids by Opener

When should you bid again as the opening bidder? Mental arithmetic to the rescue.

If partner has raised, or responded in no-trumps, the opening bidder has a pretty good idea of the upper and lower limits of the combined values. A little addition produces two totals, one optimistic and one pessimistic. If the optimistic total (opener's points plus the most points partner could have for his response) doesn't approach the magic number of 26, you should shut up.

The only time you can't shut up is when the response is in a new suit. This forces you to rebid. With 12-14 points, you can put the damper on partner's enthusiasm by making a minimum rebid: either one no-trump, two of your suit, a raise of his suit, or a bid in a lower-ranking suit than the one opened.

With a better hand you can give him all kinds of encouragement: a jump raise in his suit, a jump in your own suit or no-trumps, or bid any new suit. Or you can proudly sit up in your chair and bid game.

Rebids by Responder

After you have made one response, should you just rest on your laurels? Not at all.

If you have 11 or 12 points in high cards (and distribution points, if there is a fit), you should respond twice because he may have substantially more than the 12 points you originally gave him credit for. Your second response may be all the encouragement he needs to go to game.

With 13-17 points, as responder you should insist on game. Make your second bid in a new suit, even a three-card suit. Partner is forced to bid again.

When you have 18 points or more, think big. You're in the slam zone. If you don't make a jump response the first time, keep naming new suits and stop short of slam only if partner keeps rebidding his original suit to discourage you.

When Partner Opens One No-trump

If your partner opens one no-trump, that shows 15-17 points. Because his hand is defined more narrowly than after an opening of one of a suit, the responses to one no-trump are slightly different from responses to a suit contract.

- Raise him to two no-trumps with 9 or 10 points (with 17 points, or 16 points and a five-card suit he should press on to three no-trumps)

- Raise him to three no-trumps with 11 to 15 points

- Raise him to six no-trumps with 18 or 19 points.

If you have a weak distributional hand with a long suit, bid it at the two level. This is called a **weakness take-out** and partner should pass. It simply says that because you know you are facing a balanced hand you think you will make more tricks in your suit than he will in one no-trump. You could have no points at all for this action and the most you would have is 7 or 8.

If you have a stronger hand of 9 or more points with a five-card or longer major, jump in your suit and partner will choose between game in that suit and game in no-trumps. Be careful about showing minor suits; remember, that unless you are interested in a slam, or have extreme distribution, it is more likely that three no-trumps will be the easiest game.

Competitive bidding

Competitive describes bidding that involves both partnerships. If your opponents open the bidding there is no need to go quietly.

Overcalls

You can overcall at the one or two level, depending on whether or not your suit outranks the opponent's suit. This is undoubtedly the most dangerous bid in Bridge. This is because once your opponent has made a bid, his partner has a fair idea of the strength of the combined hands. With strength and length in the suit you have bid, it is easy to double you.

Beginners – and even experienced players – are much better off reserving the overcall for hands that contain a good, long suit.

Take-out Double

If you have 12 points or so with no good suit but support for all the unbid suits, you can double at your first opportunity to bid, provided partner has not already bid. This is known as a **take-out double**, and it forces your partner to take your double out by naming his longest and strongest suit or bidding no-trumps. Your partner may pass only if he is *certain* that your side can defeat the contract. With 10 points or more, he should bid one level higher than necessary. This jump bid should alert you to the possibility that the two of you might have a game.

One No-trump Overcall

To bid one no-trump after an opponent has opened the bidding you need more or less the same as to open one no-trump, but you do need a good stopper in the suit opened.

Pass

If you have opening values but your hand does not fit into any of the above categories, then it is perfectly all right to pass and hope either that your partner has something and can make a bid of his own or that your opponents will bid too high or butcher the play of the hand.

Penalty Doubles

On the first round of the bidding, a double is for take-out (see above). In other situations, a double is for penalties. A **penalty double** says that you think the opponents are going down in their contract and the stakes are doubled. Partner should pass the double except with a particularly wild hand.

The best time to double is when you have good trumps, particularly when you are sitting over declarer, i.e. the player on your right has bid the suit and you are strong in it. In addition, either you need some general defensive strength (remember that aces and kings are more likely to score than queens and jacks), or else you expect partner to hold some strength perhaps because he has opened the bidding. A singleton in the suit partner has opened is also useful because you might be able to score some ruffs.

In doubling a no-trump contract, it's best to have a long suit where you are missing only one or two of the top honours and sure-fire tricks on the side that will give you a chance to win the lead in order to cash the established cards in your long suit.

Redoubles

Any contract that is doubled, whether for take-out or for penalties, can be redoubled, which doubles the score yet again. A **redouble** of a take-out double tends to show all-round high cards, while a redouble of a penalty double shows that you think the doubler is wrong!

Magic Numbers

If your points, added to the points you think your partner has, total 26, bid like a lion. If the total is probably less than 26, it's usually safer to bid like a mouse.

If you and your partner have a good chance of having a total of 33 points between you, bid as bravely as a wild bull elephant. You probably have a slam.

The Bidding Can Affect the Play

When we looked at the play of the hand earlier (see page 18) we were playing MiniBridge, so there was no bidding. However, in Bridge every contract is arrived at after an auction, which gives information to all four players and this information can have a significant effect on the play.

Offence

In offence, whether you are playing Bridge or MiniBridge you are always in possession of important information, derived either from the bidding (in Bridge) or from the announcement (in MiniBridge).

An example deal is shown on the next page.

North

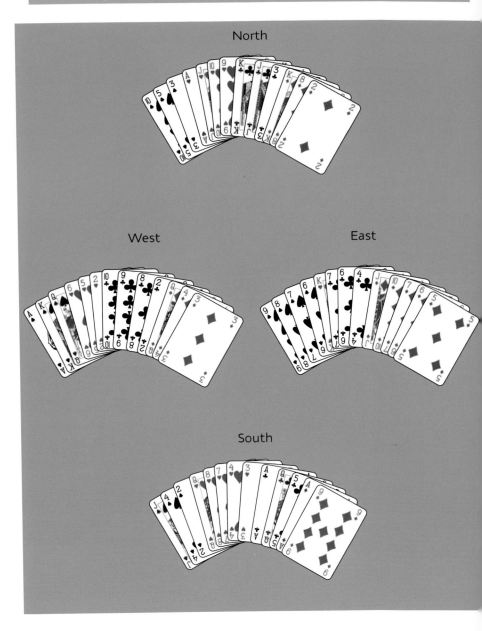

West

East

South

The bidding is:

West	North	East	South
Pass	1 ♣	Pass	1 ♥
Pass	2 ♥	Pass	4 ♥
All pass			

West passes as dealer and North, with no five-card major and not enough points to open one no-trump, opens one club. This is sometimes known as a **prepared club**. East does not have enough to bid and South responds one heart. This bid in a new suit is *forcing* – North must not pass. With four-card support for hearts, North raises to two hearts, and, with a hand that is worth an opening bid himself, South goes straight to game, i.e. bids four hearts.

West's spade holding is a perfect choice for an opening lead, and he starts with the ace of spades, followed by the king and queen of spades, all of which win tricks. West then plays the 10 of clubs, won by South with the queen.

On page 26 we looked at the finesse, and in normal circumstances South would hope that West held the king of hearts. South would play a low heart from hand, playing the 9 from dummy if West were to follow with a low card, thus avoiding the loss of a heart trick when West held the king.

But the situation here is different because South already knows that West holds 9 high-card points in spades, and West passed as dealer, so can't hold the king of hearts because that would give him 12 high-card points.

Accordingly, declarer plays a heart to the ace, the only chance being that East holds the singleton king. When East's king drops, South makes four hearts.

Note that in MiniBridge everyone would have declared their point-count so South would have known that West held 11 high-card points, and that again there was no room for him to hold the king of hearts.

Defence

Opening Leads

On page 19 we looked at some criteria for choosing an opening lead. In MiniBridge you have information about everyone's high-card points, much more information than in Bridge. However, in Bridge you learn more about the distribution and about the likely location of those high cards.

In addition to the suggestions made earlier, some other suitable candidates for opening lead can be added:

- **Lead your partner's suit.** If you have three worthless cards in it (6, 5, 3), lead the highest (6) against a no-trump contract, or the middle card (5) against a trump contract. If you have a doubleton honour (queen, 6), lead the honour (queen). If you have three cards or more with an honour in his suit (queen, 6, 5), lead your lowest card (5).

- **Lead an unbid suit.** Sometimes when the opponents fail to mention a particular suit in their bidding it can indicate a serious shortage of strength there. If your partner has any high cards at all they are most likely to be in this suit.

General Defensive Strategy

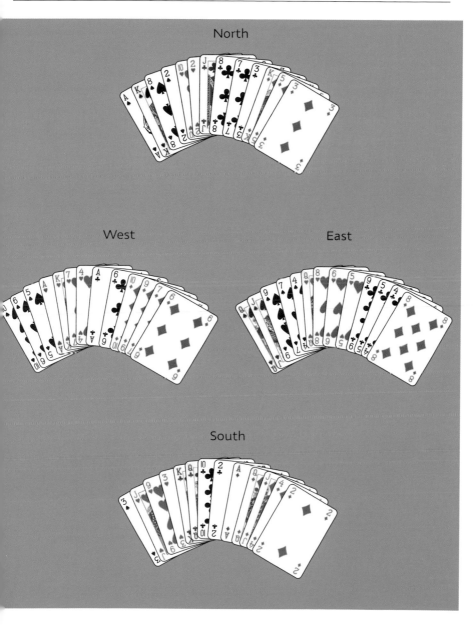

West	North	East	South
			1 ♦
Pass	1 ♠	Pass	2 ♣
Pass	3 ♣	All pass	

South is dealer and opens one diamond. West does not have enough to bid, and North responds one spade, trying to see if there is an eight-card fit in that suit. East passes and South shows his second suit by rebidding two clubs. This is one of the few rebids that is **unlimited**, i.e. South could have a minimum or a very strong hand. With 11 high-card points North has enough to **invite game**, so raises South's second suit. However, this time South is minimum and passes.

West has an attractive lead in the unbid suit, so leads the ace of hearts. However, when dummy comes down with three diamonds, West realises that South is likely to have five diamonds (with only four, most of the time he would have a balanced hand and therefore rebid one no-trump) and so East is likely to have a singleton. Accordingly, at trick two West switches to a diamond. After winning the diamond, the best South can do is play a trump. West wins his ace, and plays another diamond for East to ruff. East then puts West in with the king of hearts to get a second diamond ruff to beat three clubs.

West has been able to find this dynamic defence only because of the bidding. Simply knowing that East held 5 high-card points, as in MiniBridge, would not have helped at all.

Scoring

Y ou learn scoring best through experience, so skim through this
section to get an idea of the principles, then use it for reference.
You will find there are some terms we have not yet explained,
but all will become clear as you continue.

Bridge is played in rubbers. A **rubber** is the best of three games.

Winning a Game

As explained on page 41, when you and your partner get 100 points or
more below the line before your opponents do, you win a game and
you draw a line under your 100 points or more.

You score these points below the line by succeeding in bid contracts,
i.e. by scoring contract points:

- If your contract is in clubs or diamonds, you get 20 points below
the line for each trick that you bid for and make.

- If your contract is in hearts or spades, you get 30 points below
the line.

- If your contract is in no-trumps, you get 40 points below the line
for the first trick and 30 points for each additional trick you bid
for and make.

Remember: you don't have to make your 100 points all at once. You
can bid and make two spades on one hand (60 points below the line);
then on a later hand (if the opponents haven't made 100 points in the
meantime) you can bid and make one no-trump or two of anything
else that adds up to 40 or more points.

You are then **vulnerable** and you start all over again trying to score
another 100 points or more below the line. If you succeed, you win a
rubber.

Winning a Rubber

If you win two games before your opponents win a game, you get a bonus score of 700 points.

If your opponents win a game before you make your second game, you get only a 500-point bonus score.

Vulnerability Affects the Score

If you have not yet made a game in the rubber, you are **non-vulnerable**; if you have made a game in the rubber you are vulnerable.

- If you're not vulnerable and you fail to make your contract, the **penalty** or bonus points that your opponents collect is 50 points for each trick short of your contract. If they double you, they collect 100 points for the first trick you're down, 200 points for the next two tricks after the first one and 300 points for any subsequent trick.

- If you're vulnerable, going down costs you 100 points a trick undoubled and a whopping 200 points for the first trick doubled. Each doubled trick after the first one costs an additional 300 points.

- If you're unlucky enough to redouble and go down, you just double the ordinary doubled score.

- Other points that go above the line are the ones you get for making more tricks than your contract called for. Your overtricks don't count towards game, but they're worth 20 each if your contract was clubs or diamonds and 30 points each if your contract was hearts, spades or no-trumps.

- If you're doubled, you score double for the tricks you contracted for. If you make extra tricks, each one counts 100 points not vulnerable and 200 points vulnerable. If you redouble, each extra trick counts twice as much: 200 not vulnerable; 400 vulnerable. You also get 50 extra points for the 'insult' when you make a doubled or redoubled contract.

- If you're doubled in, say, two hearts and make it, as well as 50 for the insult, you score twice 60, i.e. 120 points, which is all below the line, and counts as game just like any other. This is called **doubled into game**. Before you make such a double, you need to be very confident that your opponents are going down.

Slam Bonuses

You get extra bonus points for bidding and making a slam. A small slam (all the tricks but one bid and made) gets you a bonus of 500 points not vulnerable, 750 points vulnerable. A grand slam (all the tricks bid and made) gets you 1,000 points not vulnerable, 1,500 points vulnerable.

Honours

Honours also get you extra points above the line. If one player (even one of your opponents) has four of the highest five cards in your trump suit (such as ace, king, jack, 10), his side gets 100 points. All five of the highest cards in a trump suit (ace, king, queen, jack, 10) in one hand are worth 150 points. All four aces in one hand at a no-trump contract are also worth 150 points.

Winning the Rubber

Remember: a rubber ends as soon as you or your opponents win two games, and the bonus is either 500 or 700 as explained earlier.

If you don't have time to finish a rubber, if one side has a game and the other hasn't, the game is worth 300 points above the line.

The Score Card

Here is a sample score card:

WE	THEY
	500^8
100^5	750^7
30^5	30^3
30^1	300^2
60^1	100^3
40^4	
90^5	
60^6	180^7

At the top of the left-hand side of the paper goes the word 'We'. All the points you and your partner make go on this side of the vertical line.

On the right-hand side of the line goes the word 'They', and all the opponents' points go on this side of the vertical line.

The thick central horizontal line is very important. It separates the contract points – the ones you bid for, which go below the line – from the points you didn't bid for, which go above the line.

The score sheet illustrated above is for the following rubber (viewed from North/South's perspective):

1 Deal 1: North/South bid two hearts and made it with an overtrick.

2 Deal 2: North/South bid three spades, were doubled and went down two tricks.

3 Deal 3: East/West bid three no-trumps and made an overtrick.

4 Deal 4: North/South bid one no-trump and made it exactly.

5 Deal 5: North/South bid three spades and made an overtrick. North held the ace, king, queen and 10, so scored 100 for honours.

6 Deal 6: North/South bid three clubs and made it exactly.

7 Deal 7: East/West bid and made six spades.

8 East/West scored 500 points for winning a three-game rubber.

If you add all that up you will find that North/South scored 410 points to East/West's 1,860 points. So the total was 1,450 points. That would usually be rounded down (in the UK; the practice in the US is to round up) and divided by 100 so here East/West won a 14-point rubber. If they were playing for a stake, such as 1p a hundred, or £15 a hundred, they would have won 14p or £210, depending on the agreement.

Scoring Reference Guide

If you play with a new pack of cards there is usually a handy Bridge scoring guide included. The following should help you work out the scores for overtricks and **undertricks**.

Overtricks

	Not vulnerable	Vulnerable
Undoubled, each	Trick value	Trick value
Doubled, each	100	200
Redoubled, each	200	400
Making doubled or redoubled contract	50	50

Penalties for Undertricks

	Not Vulnerable		Vulnerable	
	Undoubled	Doubled	Undoubled	Doubled
1 down	50	100	100	200
2 down	100	300	200	500
3 down	150	500	300	800
4 down	200	800	400	1,100
5 down	250	1,100	500	1,400
6 down	300	1,400	600	1,700
7 down	350	1,700	700	2,000

If redoubled, multiply the doubled values by two.

The Language of Bridge

I f you know the terminology, you can soon begin to sound like an expert. The words marked with an asterisk are not actually covered in this book but I have included them in case you hear other people use them.

Auction: the bidding. The conversation that takes place before the play of the hand in order to decide the contract. A review of the auction simply means: 'Who bid what?'

Balance*: a bid to reopen the bidding when your opponents' bidding shows weakness. You can often balance after two passes with as few as 10 high-card points.

Balanced hand: a hand in which the suits are fairly evenly distributed, such as 4-3-3-3. A balanced hand is defined as not having a singleton or void and having no more than one doubleton.

Below the line: a term used to describe points scored by making a bid contract. These points are scored below a horizontal line on a score card.

Better minor: a conventional bid whereby an opening in a minor suit may be made on a three-card suit in a balanced hand that is out of range for a one no-trump opening.

Bid: an educated guess as to how much your hand is worth on offence. You can bid – depending on your cards and courage – any number from one to seven of spades, hearts, diamonds, clubs or no-trumps. If your hand is worthless, you may pass. If you think your opponents are in deep water with their bid, you may double. They can redouble, also. Some doubles have a special meaning (*see* Double). Some bids have an unusual meaning (*see* Convention).

Bidding: *see* Auction

Blackwood*: a sudden bid of four no-trumps that requests your partner to indicate the number of aces in his hand by responding as follows: with no aces or all four, five clubs; with one ace, five diamonds;

with two aces, five hearts; with three aces, five spades. Kings are indicated in the same way after partner bids five no-trumps.

Cash: to lead a winning card.

Contract: the partnership that makes the highest bid *contracts* for a specific number of tricks (tricks won after the partnership wins the first six tricks). Their final bid becomes the contract.

Convention: any bid or play that has a special or unusual meaning agreed to by a partnership. Blackwood is an example because four no-trumps indicates a request for aces – a special meaning – rather than a desire to play the hand in four no-trumps. The meaning of a conventional bid must be disclosed to the opponents.

Cover: playing a higher-ranking card than one your opponent has led. You cover a queen with a king, for instance.

Cross-ruff: trumping different suits back and forth from your hand to your partner's. When you are caught in a cross-ruff, the opponents do it to you.

Cue-bid: a surprise bid of one of the opponents' suits or a surprise bid in any suit after the trump suit has been agreed upon. It usually indicates an ace or a void in the suit bid, but could be a singleton or king.

Cut: you cut for partners and to see who is to be dealer by each taking a few cards from a pack and seeing whose is the highest; you cut before dealing in order to ensure that a card-sharp dealer does not give himself a good hand.

Dealer: the player who distributes the cards.

Declarer: the player who winds up playing the contract with his partner as dummy.

Declaring side: the side, North/South or East/West, who are declarer/dummy.

Defence: the part of the game where you try to defeat your opponents' contract. *See* Offence.

Defender: not declarer or dummy; one of the players trying to defeat declarer's contract.

Defending side: the side, North/South or East/West, who are trying to defeat declarer's contract and are not declarer or dummy.

Denomination: a word that embraces no-trumps as well as all four suits.

Discard: a card (usually worthless) other than a trump or the suit led.

Distribution points: the points you add to your high-card points in estimating the value of your hand. They apply only when you have a fit for partner.

Double: a two-edged sword. It can be an attempt to penalise your opponents (penalty, or business, double) or it can be an invitation to your partner to bid (take-out double).

Doubled into game: This occurs when your doubled score below the line is over 100, taking you to game.

Doubleton: two cards in a suit.

Down: going down means failing to make your contract, e.g. three down means falling three tricks short of the contract.

Draw: as in *drawing* trumps, i.e. leading a suit often enough to extract the opponents' cards in that suit. This is also known as 'pulling' trumps.

Drop: you drop an opponent's king, for example, if you play your ace and the poor wretch had a singleton king. Sometimes it takes two or three leads of a suit to drop an opponent's high card.

Duck: a move whereby you pass up your first opportunity to take a trick. This can cut the communications between your opponents' hands.

Dummy: the hand that is exposed on the table once the contract has been established.

Duplicate*: a form of tournament Bridge, whereby the cards are kept as dealt in slotted boards and played again by other players. This way you can compare scores on any given hand. This greatly reduces the luck element.

Endplay*: giving one of your opponents a trick at such a time when he will be forced to make a lead that benefits you.

Entry: a trump or a high card that provides transportation from your hand to your partner's or vice versa.

Finesse: a way a smaller card can sneak past a larger card and win a trick. You finesse a king by leading toward an ace-queen combination. If the king is on your left and your opponent doesn't play it, your queen will win the trick – the simplest form of a finesse.

Follow suit: playing a card in the same suit led by you or the opponents – a *must* if you have one.

Forcing bid: a bid that forces your partner to respond unless he wants his head bitten off. A **cue-bid** whereby you bid the same suit your opponents have bid, is forcing upon your partner. Many conventional bids force a response. If you open two clubs, for instance, your partner must respond even with absolute rubbish in his hand... in which case he bids two diamonds to put a damper on your enthusiasm.

Game: 100 points or more scored below the line.

Good fit: hand that makes meeting a target likely.

Hand: the thirteen cards dealt to a particular player.

High cards: usually aces, kings, queens and jacks, but sometimes a 3 can be a high card if it captures an opponent's 2.

High-card points: an aid to hand evaluation: count 4 for an ace, 3 for a king, 2 for a queen and 1 for a jack.

Honour: an ace, king, queen, jack or 10.

Honours: bonus points for special holdings. With four honours in a suit you score 100 points above the line. Five honours in a suit or all four aces in a no-trump contract gets you 150 points above the line. The only catch is that the final contract *must* be in the denomination with the honours for you to get credit for these bonus points.

Informative double*: *see* Take-out double.

Interior/internal sequence: a sequence including honour cards such as ace, jack, 10 or queen, 10, 9, where you have two touching honours, and also a higher honour that is not touching.

Invite game: make a bid that asks partner to bid game if he has more than a minimum opener.

Jump: any response or overcall that is at least one level higher than need be.

Jump shift: a single jump in a new suit by the responder to show a strong hand.

Lead: the play of the first card on a trick.

Long card: a card of a suit left in your hand after your opponents are exhausted in that suit.

Long suit: suit of which you hold five or more cards.

Major suits: hearts and spades.

MiniBridge: a form of Bridge that can be played in its own right or used for teaching purposes; it is a form of Bridge that works without any bidding.

Minor suits: diamonds and clubs.

Newspaper hand: a hand that is tricky enough to rate comment by your favourite newspaper's Bridge columnist. The following is a typical one:

Dealer North   Both Vulnerable

```
                              NORTH
                              ♠ A K J
                              ♥ 10 8 6
                              ♦ K Q
                              ♣ K 9 8 3 2
WEST                                                          EAST
♠ 10 8 6 3                                                    ♠ Q 9 7
♥ 5 4 2                                                       ♥ 3
♦ A J 8 5 4 3                                                 ♦ 9 7 6 2
♣ none                                                        ♣ Q 7 6 5 4
                              SOUTH
                              ♠ 5 4 2
                              ♥ A K Q J 9 7
                              ♦ 10
                              ♣ A J 10
```

West	North	East	South
	1NT	Pass	6♥
All Pass			

Opening lead ♦ A

The tricky part of this hand is discarding a club on dummy's diamond king when it wins the second trick. After drawing trumps, South leads the ace of clubs, then the jack of clubs and overtakes it with dummy's king. When West discards, South knows East has the queen, so then leads the 9 of clubs. If East covers with the queen, South trumps, gets back to dummy with a high spade and discards his losing spade on the now-good 8 of clubs. If East ducks the 9 of clubs, South pitches his losing spade instantly.

No-trumps: in a contract that is played without trumps the highest card played in the suit led wins the trick.

Non-vulnerable: before your side has won a game you are non-vulnerable; if you go down in a contract you lose fewer points than if you were vulnerable.

Offence: the act of declarership; the opposite of defence.

Opening bid: the first bid by anybody at the table.

Opening lead: the first card played to the first trick.

Overcall: a bid made over an opponent's bid by the side that did not open.

Overtrick: any trick in excess of the ones you contracted for.

Partscore: any score less than 100 points (*see* Game) bid and made in one deal. In rubber Bridge, partscores are extremely important. Two of them can easily add up to game.

Pass: usually a pessimistic bid to warn your partner that your hand isn't worth shouting about.

Penalty: the cost of failure to make your contract. Penalties are scored above the line and don't count toward making game.

Penalty double: a double that means you think they are going down. See page 64 for just how many points you collect if you defeat your opponents' doubled contract. The penalties can be staggering.

Pinning: preventing a card from achieving its potential.

Pre-emptive bids*: these bids involve bidding as high as you can as fast as you can with a hand that's long in one suit but not very strong in high cards. Chances are that you'll be set, but chances are equally good that your opponents have game and won't be able to find it because you have crowded them out of several chances to bid at a low level. You may lose 200 or 300 points, but it's much better than letting them make 600 or 800 points (game and rubber).

Prepared club: bidding a three-card club suit when you have a balanced hand with no five-card major.

Raise: bidding to a higher level in a suit your partner named first.

Rank: describes the relative importance of the suits and no-trumps: no-trumps ranks highest, then spades, hearts, diamonds and finally clubs.

Redouble: a way of indicating to your partner that your opponents have made a bad double and that you have either a good hand or a good chance of making your contract.

Revoke*: the unpardonable crime of not following suit when you could have. Usually penalised by two tricks that you have to hand back to your opponents.

Riffle-shuffle: the best form of shuffle whereby the pack is divided into roughly two halves, which are then held face down and bent up with one or two cards from each side being released at a time, in order to mix up the two halves. This type of shuffle is much more efficient than the alternative of loosely holding one half in each hand and attempting to mix them vertically.

Rubber: the first partnership to score two games wins the rubber, thus scoring extra points.

Ruff: ruff means to trump (*see* Trump).

Sacrifice*: a semi-suicidal bid whereby you contract for more tricks than you can possibly make. A sacrifice bid generally pays off if the penalty points collected by the opponents add up to less than they could have made by playing and making their own contract.

Set: same as defeat. You set the opponents when you defeat their contract.

Singleton: one card in a suit.

Slam: a contract for twelve (small slam) or all thirteen tricks (grand slam).

Squeeze play*: an advanced play, whereby you give one or both of your opponents an impossible choice of discards.

Stayman*: a conventional bid made in response to an opening no-trump bid. In its simplest version, responder bids two clubs, which requests the opening no-trump bidder to bid a four-card major suit if he has one. Otherwise opener bids two diamonds and it's up to responder to determine where the contract is to be played.

Strip: to exhaust a hand of a particular suit by leading it repeatedly.

Suit contract: a contract where the final bid has been in spades, hearts, diamonds or clubs, i.e. not in no-trumps.

Suits: spades, hearts, diamonds, clubs.

Take-out double: a double of the opponents' bid, usually at your first opportunity to bid. Also known as an informative double, because it informs your partner that you have a decent hand and that you'd like to hear from him.

Tenace: the best and third-best cards in a suit in one hand, such as ace, queen; these can be lower cards when the higher ones have already been played.

Trick: in Bridge a trick comprises four cards, one contributed by each of the four players.

Trump: a trump is a card in the suit named in the final contract; to trump (or ruff) means playing a card in this suit if you can't follow suit.

Undertricks: the number of tricks that fall short of your contract when you're set.

Unlimited: an adjective usually used to describe a bid that could be strong or weak.

Void: having no cards in a particular suit.

Vulnerable: once your side has won a game you are vulnerable, i.e. vulnerable to higher penalties for reckless bidding.

Weakness take-out: a simple bid in a suit after a one no-trump opening. This can be made with a very weak hand and opener should pass.

Yarborough*: a hand with no card higher than a 9. Named after Lord Yarborough who offered 1,000 to 1 odds before dealing that the taker would not be dealt such a miserable hand. The actual odds against such a hand are much higher, so the wily old gentleman made a tidy sum from this bet.

A Little Private Practice

Here are some do-it-yourself exercises on just a few of the basic things you need to know to be a good player.

Point Counting

How many points are these hands worth if you have the chance to open the bidding?

1. ♠ A 6 5
   ♥ K Q 10 3
   ♦ K 5
   ♣ Q J 10 2

2. ♠ Q J
   ♥ K J 2
   ♦ 3 2
   ♣ A J 7 6 5 4

3. ♠ A K 10 9 8 7
   ♥ Q J 5
   ♦ 3
   ♣ 9 8 6

4. ♠ K 7
   ♥ A K Q 7 6 3
   ♦ A 6 3
   ♣ 8 2

5. ♠ K 9 8 6
   ♥ Q 8 7
   ♦ K J
   ♣ A 7 6 2

6. ♠ A K J
   ♥ A Q 10 9
   ♦ 10 9
   ♣ K J 10 9

7. ♠ A Q 10 9 8
   ♥ Q J 10
   ♦ A K 10 9
   ♣ A

Answers

1. 15 points in high cards. This is the minimum needed for opening one no-trump, but these are 'good' points. 4-4-3-2 distribution is better than 4-3-3-3 because you have two possible sources of tricks. Holding 10s (and 9s) in suits where you also hold honours often enables you to make more tricks. Here you have two 10s. Queens and jacks are more likely to make tricks when they are held in combination with other honour cards.

2. 12 points in high cards. While this is a comfortable opening bid (you need only 10 points when you have a six-card suit), these are 'poor' points. If your opponents hold the ace-king of spades, your queen-jack will be worthless. You have no 10s and 9s. Don't panic: bid one club, but don't expect miracles unless your partner responds with enthusiasm.

3. You have only 10 points in high cards, but this is worth opening, because you have a good six-card suit.

4. 16 points and a very good six-card suit. Open one heart, intending to make a jump rebid of three hearts next time.

5. 13 points in a balanced hand: a curate's egg – good in parts. The 4-4-3-2 distribution and only one jack (and that is with another honour) is good, but the scarcity of 10s and 9s is bad. In all, an average 13-count. With no five-card major, open your better minor: one club.

6. 18 'good' points in high cards, too good to open one no-trump. With no five-card major open one club and rebid two no-trumps to show 18 or 19 points. This hand is worth more than its bare 18 because: 4-4-3-2 distribution is better than 4-3-3-3; look at all those 10s and 9s; and the honour cards are all held in combination with other honour cards. In particular, there are no unsupported queens and jacks.

7. 20 high-card points. This is just enough to open two spades. If your partner responds two no-trumps, rebid three diamonds and leave the rest to him.

Responses

Your partner made an opening bid of one heart. What do you respond with each of these hands?

1. ♠ K 3
    ♥ A 5 3
    ♦ J 10 7 6
    ♣ 9 8 4 3

2. ♠ A 8
    ♥ 5 4 3 2
    ♦ K 10 9
    ♣ Q J 10 8

3. ♠ A K Q 6 5
    ♥ 4 3 2
    ♦ 5 4 3 2
    ♣ 10

4. ♠ 5 4 3
    ♥ Q 3 2
    ♦ A J 10 9 5
    ♣ A 5

5. ♠ 7
    ♥ 10 9 7 6 4
    ♦ A K 9 8
    ♣ 10 9 8

6. ♠ Q 9 7
    ♥ 8 6
    ♦ A Q 10 8
    ♣ 10 9 8 6

7. ♠ A Q 10 8
    ♥ 8 6
    ♦ Q 9 7
    ♣ 10 9 8 6

8. ♠ 7 5
    ♥ 8 6
    ♦ A Q 10 7 6 2
    ♣ J 10 3

9. ♠ A Q 10 8
    ♥ 8 6
    ♦ 5 2
    ♣ K J 10 5 2

10. ♠ A K Q
    ♥ 10 9 8
    ♦ A K J 10 9
    ♣ Q 10

Answers

1. Bid two hearts. The simple raise will give him some mild encouragement.

2. Bid three hearts, a double raise. This shows him at least three-card trump support and 10-12 points.

3. Bid one spade. This is more informative than just raising his suit. Besides, your heart support is nothing to brag about and the quality of your spades is very good.

4. Bid three hearts. Here, where your suit is a minor, it is better to raise his five-card major immediately. You know you have an eight-card heart fit so there is no point in looking for a minor-suit fit.

5. Bid four hearts, a triple raise. With your singleton, your trump support and your good diamonds, you should have an excellent go at game. If you get set, be comforted in the almost certain knowledge that your opponents missed a game in spades or possibly in clubs.

6. Bid one no-trump. You have 8 high-card points, more than enough to make sure your partner gets another chance to bid.

7. Respond one spade. The same hand as before, but this time you can bid your four-card suit at the one level. To respond one no-trump to one heart denies four spades.

8. Respond one no-trump. You need at least 10 points to bid at the two level, so this hand is not strong enough. If your partner were to rebid two clubs, you could bid two diamonds to show a weak hand with a long suit.

9. Bid one spade. Although you have the 10 points necessary to bid at the two level, you are not strong enough to force to game, which is what you would do if you bid two clubs and then two spades. If you don't bid your spades on the first round you may miss a 4-4 fit there, and bidding is mostly about finding a 4-4 major-suit fit.

10. Bid three diamonds. Think big. You have 19 high-card points, which should put your partnership into the slam zone. Tell him the good news by jumping in a new suit (a jump shift).

Overcalls and Take-out Doubles

The opponent on your right has opened one heart. What do you bid with each of these hands?

1. ♠ A K Q J 10 2
  ♥ 4 3 2
  ♦ 7 5
  ♣ 8 7

2. ♠ A J 10 2
  ♥ 2
  ♦ Q J 10 9
  ♣ A J 7 2

3. ♠ K J 9 8 6
  ♥ 4
  ♦ K J 9 4
  ♣ 8 7 3

The opponent on your right opens one spade; what do you bid with each of these hands?

4. ♠ A J 10
  ♥ Q J 10 9 8 7
  ♦ K 3 2
  ♣ 2

5. ♠ K J 6
  ♥ A 10
  ♦ K Q J 10 4
  ♣ K 10 2

6. ♠ 4 3
  ♥ K J 8 7 2
  ♦ K Q 8 7
  ♣ K 7

Answers

1. Bid one spade. With 10 points and a six-card suit you have a sound overcall. It is worth taking a few risks when you have 150 honours.

2. Make a take-out double. You want your partner to bid his best suit. With 10 or more points he should jump the bidding. The most likely game for your side is four spades – if he jumps to two spades, make a try for game by raising to three spades.

3. Overcall one spade. Even though you wouldn't have opened the bidding, you are strong enough for a minimum one-level overcall. Maybe overcalling will help partner with his opening lead; maybe your partner will be able to raise spades, perhaps making it harder for your opponents or enabling you to find a spade contract your way.

4. Bid two hearts. Even though you are missing the ace and king of your suit, the rest of the suit is solid.

5. Overcall one no-trump. This shows the same values as opening one no-trump. Your partner will add his points to your 15–17 and bid to the right level. You should accept any invitational bid he makes.

6. Pass. Discretion is the better part of valour with this bad a hand. If you bid two hearts with such a poor suit, your left-hand opponent might be able to take a huge penalty if he has length and strength in hearts. It is advisable to have a six-card suit to overcall at the two level.

How Should These Hands be Bid?

Look at the three pairs of hands below and work out how you think the bidding should have gone. In each case the dealer is West.

1. West
   ♠ A 5
   ♥ K Q J 5 3
   ♦ J 2
   ♣ K 10 9 4

   East
   ♠ K Q 10 6
   ♥ 4
   ♦ A Q 9 4 3
   ♣ 8 3 2

2. West
   ♠ A K 8 7 3
   ♥ K Q 9 8
   ♦ 7 3
   ♣ 8 2

   East
   ♠ 9 2
   ♥ A J 10 3
   ♦ A K 9 8
   ♣ 10 6 3

3. West
   ♠ A Q J 10 9 5
   ♥ K 4 2
   ♦ 7
   ♣ Q 7 6

   East
   ♠ K 2
   ♥ A Q 3
   ♦ A J 8 6 5
   ♣ A 8 3

Answers

1. West
   1 ♥
   2 ♣
   3 NT

   East
   1 ♠
   2 NT
   Pass

East is not strong enough to bid diamonds then spades because that sequence is forcing to game, so he starts by responding one spade. West bids his second suit and East bids two no-trumps, inviting game in no-trumps. With 14 high-card points, West has enough to accept.

2. West
   1 ♠
   2 ♥
   Pass

   East
   2 ♦
   4 ♥

East responds in his lowest four-card suit at the two level. When West shows his hearts, East must jump to game with 12 'good' high-card points.

Incidentally, how would you play four hearts on a trump lead? This is another example of a cross-ruff just like we saw earlier. Cash the ace-kings of spades and diamonds, and cross-ruff spades and diamonds. You will make eleven tricks.

3.
West	East
1 ♠	2 ♦
2 ♠	3 ♣
4 ♠	6 ♠
Pass	

Although East has enough high-card points for a jump response of three diamonds, this shows either a better suit, or else a better fit with partner. Two diamonds is forcing, so there is no need to worry about West passing.

West rebids two spades and East is still interested in a slam, so it would be premature to close the auction with a bid of three no-trumps or four spades. Any new suit by East is forcing here, so East should bid three clubs to try to get more information.

West's spades are so good that they do not need any support from East. West gets that message across by jumping to four spades.

That is all the encouragement East needs. With a spade honour and such good controls, he jumps straight to slam.

Again, let us look at the play. Say North leads a trump. West's best chance is to set up dummy's diamonds. Failing that he may have to lead up to the queen of clubs, hoping that South has the king. West should win the spade in hand, play a diamond to the ace, ruff a diamond and then play a spade to dummy's king. Provided both opponents follow to the king of spades, West ruffs another diamond. If both opponents follow, West draws the last trump, crosses to dummy with a heart and ruffs another diamond, setting up the fifth one for a club discard. If either spades or diamonds fail to break favourably, then West just draws trumps, crosses to the ace of clubs and leads a low club towards his queen, making when South has the king.

Playing No-trump Contracts

1. North (dummy)

♠ K 3
♥ Q 8 6
♦ A Q 9 3 2
♣ 5 4 3

South (you)

♠ A 6 5
♥ A K 5
♦ J 10 8 5
♣ A Q 6

You are the declarer in three no-trumps. Your left-hand opponent makes the opening lead of the spade queen. How do you play the hand?

2. North (dummy)

♠ A 3
♥ Q J 10 9 8 7
♦ 5 4 3
♣ K 2

South (you)

♠ K 5 4 2
♥ 3 2
♦ A K Q
♣ A 5 4 3

You are declarer in three no-trumps, and your left-hand opponent leads the diamond jack. How do you play the hand?

3. North (dummy)
   ♠ 9 8
   ♥ A K 3
   ♦ 9 8 4 2
   ♣ A 10 3 2

   South (you)
   ♠ A 4 3
   ♥ Q 5 2
   ♦ K Q J 10 3
   ♣ K 6

You are the declarer in three no-trumps. Your left-hand opponent makes the opening lead of the spade king. How do you play the hand?

4. North (dummy)
   ♠ K 10 5 4
   ♥ 10 5 4
   ♦ A 9 8 6
   ♣ A K

   South (you)
   ♠ A 3
   ♥ A 7 2
   ♦ K J 10 4 2
   ♣ J 7 2

You are declarer in three no-trumps, and your left-hand opponent leads the king of hearts. How do you play the hand?

Answers

1. You have seven sure tricks in top cards. You must find two more to make your contract. The diamond suit will provide these tricks, even if your right-hand opponent holds the diamond king, but you might as well try the finesse anyway. Win the first trick in your hand and lay down the diamond jack. If your left-hand opponent has the king and does not play it, play a small diamond from dummy. After your jack has won the trick, play the diamond 10 for another finesse. If the finesse loses and your right-hand opponent returns a club, you might as well try the queen (another finesse). If it loses, you make ten tricks; if it wins, eleven.

2. You have seven top tricks. You are lucky that your opponents didn't lead clubs or spades, the suits in which you have only two stoppers. This gives you what the experts call timing on the hand. You have the time to develop your long suit (hearts) before the opponents can develop their tricks in the black suits (spades and clubs). Because they led diamonds, you have a chance to drive out the ace and king of hearts. You must do this immediately. No matter what they return after winning these tricks, you can stop the suit. The two top hearts are all you need to lose. You'll make five no-trumps.

3. With just six top tricks, you have no chance of arriving at nine tricks unless you can make four diamond tricks. If you win the ace of spades and play the king of diamonds you will be OK if spades break 4-4, but will go down if, as is more likely, they don't. However, if the ace of diamonds is not in the hand with the long spades you can succeed anyway. You must **duck** the first spade. No doubt West will continue with a second spade and you must duck that, too. Win the third spade and play the king of diamonds. If you are lucky, East will win with the ace and won't have any more spades to play (or maybe they will break 4-4).

4. Seven top tricks. Once again you must duck the opening lead. If you make five diamond tricks you will make your contract in any event, but why gamble on that when you don't need to? Duck the second heart, too, and win the third (East shows out). Now, to make *three* no-trumps you need only nine tricks, so four diamond tricks will do, to go with two spades, two clubs and a heart. As long as West does not get the lead your contract is assured, so finesse him for the queen of diamonds. After winning the third heart, lay down the king of diamonds (in case the queen is singleton), and then play a diamond to dummy's 9. If East wins the queen he doesn't have any more hearts to play and you will still succeed.

Playing in Suit Contracts

1. North (dummy)
   ♠ 8 7
   ♥ K 8 2
   ♦ A 10 8 2
   ♣ Q 10 7 2

   South (you)
   ♠ A 10 4
   ♥ A Q J 10 9
   ♦ K 7
   ♣ K 6 3

You are the declarer in four hearts. Your left-hand opponent makes the opening lead of the 3 of hearts. How do you play the hand?

2. North (dummy)
   ♠ K J 10 5 2
   ♥ 7 6
   ♦ A K 6 5 2
   ♣ 7

   South (you)
   ♠ A Q 9 8 3
   ♥ A 5
   ♦ 8 3
   ♣ Q 10 6 2

You have reached the dizzy heights of six spades. Your left-hand opponent leads the ace of clubs and switches to a heart. How do you play the hand?

3. North (dummy)
   ♠ 8 7 4 3
   ♥ 7
   ♦ K Q J 10 6 2
   ♣ 7 2

   South (you)
   ♠ A K Q 6 2
   ♥ A 10 3
   ♦ 3
   ♣ Q 8 6 3

You are the declarer in four spades. Your left-hand opponent makes the opening lead of the 2 of hearts, you play low from dummy and East plays the king. How do you play the hand?

4. North (dummy)
   ♠ K Q 6 5
   ♥ A 5
   ♦ 6 5
   ♣ K Q J 10 2

   South (you)
   ♠ A J 10 9 8 3
   ♥ 3 2
   ♦ K Q 9 8 7
   ♣ –

The bidding:

West	North	East	South
			1 ♠
Pass	3 ♣	Pass	3 ♦
Pass	3 ♠	Pass	4 ♣
Pass	4 ♥	Pass	4 ♠
Pass	6 ♠	Pass	Pass
Pass			

You are the declarer in six spades. Your left-hand opponent leads the queen of hearts. Plan the play.

5. North (dummy)
   ♠ 9 4 2
   ♥ Q J 10 4
   ♦ K Q 7
   ♣ Q 10 3

   South (you)
   ♠ A J 5
   ♥ A 5 2
   ♦ A 10 4 3
   ♣ A 9 5

You are the declarer in three no-trumps. Your left-hand opponent leads the king of spades. How do you play the hand?

A Little Private Practice

Answers

1. Count your tricks. You have nine on top: one spade, five hearts, two diamonds and a club. You might make a second club trick if West has the jack. However, a much safer way to make that extra trick is to ruff a spade in the dummy. Win the trump lead and play ace and another spade. No doubt the defenders will continue trumps, but you win in hand and ruff your losing spade. Now cross back to hand with the king of diamonds to draw trumps and set up a club trick for your contract.

2. You have eleven tricks easily enough: five spades, one heart, two diamonds and three club ruffs in the dummy. However, to make a twelfth you will need to set up dummy's diamonds. You need diamonds to break 3-3 or 4-2. Win the heart at trick two, draw trumps in two rounds, then play the ace and king of diamonds and ruff a diamond. Ruff a club in the dummy and ruff another diamond if necessary. Ruff another club in the dummy and cash your long diamond, discarding you heart loser from hand. You can now cross-ruff the last two tricks.

3. You have a singleton in the suit led and could easily score a ruff or two in the dummy but that would be very wrong here. You can set up an awful lot of diamond tricks just by knocking out the ace. As long as trumps break 2-2 or 3-1 (about 90% of the time) you can guarantee your contract simply by winning the ace of hearts, drawing trumps and playing a diamond. Later on you can ruff something in the dummy to reach your established diamonds. If you make the mistake of ruffing a heart in dummy early on, when trumps break 3-1 you will find that you don't have an entry to your established diamonds.

4. The bidding illustrates several points you should note carefully:

   South is well worth an opening bid even though he has only 10 high-card points. A 6-5 distribution is very powerful.

   North's hand is too strong simply to raise to four spades so he makes a jump bid in his strongest outside suit. This jump in a new suit is forcing to game.

   South rebids his second suit, diamonds, just as he would have done over two clubs.

   North shows support for spades. Since the partnership is committed to game he does not have to jump. By bidding just three spades North leaves room for South to describe his hand further.

   South wants to make some encouraging move. When a major suit is agreed, all other bids are **cue-bids**, showing a control (ace,

86

king, singleton or void) in the suit bid. Normally a cue-bid in partner's suit would show a top honour rather than a shortage, but here South is a bit stuck for a bid, so he cue-bids four clubs.

North co-operates with a cue-bid of four hearts.

South has done enough now and signs off in four spades.

North is not going to give up, though, and jumps to slam.

When dummy comes down you can see that you are going to have to lose a trick to the ace of diamonds. You also need to find a parking place for your losing heart. Your only chance is to find the ace of clubs with East.

Win the ace of hearts, cash the ace and king of spades and play the king of clubs. If East plays the ace you ruff, cross back to the queen of spades and cash your three good clubs, discarding one heart and two diamonds. Now play a diamond. You may need to ruff your small diamond with dummy's last trump. If East plays low on the king of clubs, then you discard your heart straight away; if West has the ace of clubs there is nothing you could do. There is a 50% chance of your slam making. This play is called a ruffing finesse.

5. While the spade suit is not of great danger to you, it is still right to duck the king of spades, but for a slightly different reason than we have seen before. Ducking here forces West either to give you an extra spade trick (if he continues the suit), or to switch to some other suit, which is also to your advantage. If he switches to a club (perhaps most likely) that gives you a second club trick. Win in hand, cross to dummy with a diamond and run the queen of hearts. If it holds, follow with the jack of hearts. If that holds, play a club to guarantee nine tricks. If West wins a heart trick he can do you no harm. You must be able to develop a second club trick.

Defence

1. North (dummy)
   - ♠ Q 5
   - ♥ A K 5 2
   - ♦ K J 2
   - ♣ 9 8 6 4

   East (you)
   - ♠ K 10 4
   - ♥ Q 10 6 3
   - ♦ Q 6 4
   - ♣ J 7 2

   South is the declarer in three no-trumps. West leads the 3 of spades and dummy plays the 5. How do you defend?

2. North (dummy)
   - ♠ 7 6 3
   - ♥ Q 8 2
   - ♦ 8 7
   - ♣ K Q J 10 5

   East (you)
   - ♠ K 5 4
   - ♥ K J 7 4
   - ♦ 6 5 3
   - ♣ A 8 6

   South is the declarer in three no-trumps. West leads the 2 of spades, dummy plays the 3, you play the king. South wins with the ace and plays a club to dummy's king. How do you defend?

3. North (dummy)
   - ♠ 7 6 3
   - ♥ Q 8 2
   - ♦ 8 7
   - ♣ K Q J 10 5

   East (you)
   - ♠ K 5 4
   - ♥ K J 7 4
   - ♦ 6 5 3
   - ♣ A 8 6

   South is the declarer in three no-trumps. West leads the 2 of spades, dummy plays the 3, you play the king. South wins with the ace and plays a club to dummy's queen. How do you defend?

4. North (dummy)
♠ J 5 4
♥ 6
♦ A J 6 4 2
♣ K 10 4 3

East (you)
♠ 6
♥ A K 10 7 5
♦ K Q 10 7
♣ J 6 2

The bidding:

West	North	East	South
		1 ♥	1 ♠
2 ♥	3 ♠	Pass	4 ♠
Pass	Pass	Pass	

West leads the 2 of hearts. How do you defend?

5. North (dummy)
♠ 6 3 2
♥ 8 4
♦ A Q J 10 5
♣ A J 6

East (you)
♠ 8 5
♥ A Q J 10 9 3
♦ 7 4 3
♣ 8 4

The bidding:

West	North	East	South
			1 ♠
Pass	2 ♦	Pass	2 ♠
Pass	4 ♠	Pass	Pass
	Pass		

West leads the king of hearts. How do you defend?

Answers

1. You should play the 10, not the king. Your partner's lead of a low spade promises an honour so you know he has the jack or the ace or both. Let's look at a few possible layouts of the suit, because this is an important concept. If you find it difficult to follow, deal out the cards and play it through.

♠ Q 5

♠ J 8 6 3   ♠ K 10 4

♠ A 9 7 2

If you play the king declarer will make two tricks: the ace and the queen. If you play the 10 that will force his ace. When you next get in you will play the king (pinning dummy's queen) and then the 4, so partner will make his jack and 8. Partner's jack and 8 of spades here are known as a **tenace**. When you lead the 4 of spades, he has the first and third outstanding cards in the suit while declarer has the second. It is important that you have the lead, for if partner was on lead he could not play the suit without giving declarer a trick.

♠ Q 5

♠ A 8 6 3   ♠ K 10 4

♠ J 9 7 2

If you play the king and another one to partner's ace, then declarer's jack will drop your 10 and declarer will make two tricks in the suit. Even if your partner ducks the second round so declarer's queen wins, declarer can still play the jack later to pin your 10. On the other hand, if you play the 10, declarer will win with the jack. Next time you are in you play the king (**pinning** dummy's queen), and then another lead of the suit will let your partner make his ace and 8.

♠ Q 5

♠ A J 6 3   ♠ K 10 4

♠ 9 8 7 2

If you play the king, you next have to play a small card to partner's ace, and then he has to play a small card back to your 10. You cannot take four tricks immediately, and if he does not have an entry you may not be able to take four tricks at all. Compare that with playing the 10 at trick one. It holds the trick, and then you play the king and another, easily taking the first four tricks.

The only situation where it will cost you to play the 10 is when declarer started with jack doubleton. This is much less likely than all these other situations. Also, where partner leads the 2 or 3, you know that can't be the case, because with six cards headed by the ace partner would lead fourth highest, and must have two cards below the one he led.

2. This is similar to problem 3 in the section on no-trump contracts (see pages 82–83), but from the defensive perspective. If you win the ace of clubs, declarer will later be able to make all dummy's club tricks. On the other hand, if you duck until declarer is out of the suit, you can see that he will never be able to reach dummy. So duck the first two club plays, win the third and return partner's suit. Unless declarer started with four clubs, he will surely go down.

3. This is virtually the same as the previous hand but here you have the king of clubs instead of the ace. However, the principle is the same. Duck – smoothly, if you can. Declarer will now surely go back to his hand (giving you another clue as to what he holds) to take another club finesse. If he started with only two clubs he will make only one of them.

4. You can see that declarer can't hope to establish dummy's long suit, diamonds, because you have it so well held. The best thing to do is try to cut down dummy's potential to ruff hearts and switch to a trump.
   The full deal:

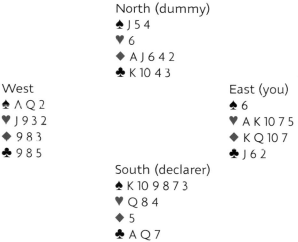

North (dummy)
♠ J 5 4
♥ 6
♦ A J 6 4 2
♣ K 10 4 3

West
♠ A Q 2
♥ J 9 3 2
♦ 9 8 3
♣ 9 8 5

East (you)
♠ 6
♥ A K 10 7 5
♦ K Q 10 7
♣ J 6 2

South (declarer)
♠ K 10 9 8 7 3
♥ Q 8 4
♦ 5
♣ A Q 7

If you switch to a trump, partner will win the queen and ace and play a third round, and declarer will be held to nine tricks.

5. If declarer needs any finesses in the minors, you know that they are working for him. The only chance is to take two trump tricks along with two hearts. You know that partner has at most a doubleton heart (he would have led low from 3 to an honour), so if he has three trumps including the ace or king and another one that can beat the 6 you are in business. Overtake the king of hearts with the ace (in case it is singleton), cash the queen of hearts and play a third round of the suit.

The full deal:

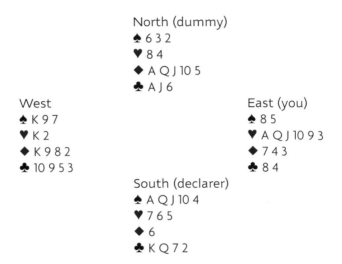

North (dummy)
♠ 6 3 2
♥ 8 4
♦ A Q J 10 5
♣ A J 6

West
♠ K 9 7
♥ K 2
♦ K 9 8 2
♣ 10 9 5 3

East (you)
♠ 8 5
♥ A Q J 10 9 3
♦ 7 4 3
♣ 8 4

South (declarer)
♠ A Q J 10 4
♥ 7 6 5
♦ 6
♣ K Q 7 2

Declarer must follow to the third round of hearts and your partner ruffs with the 7. Later the king of spades will be the setting trick.

* * *

You may have noticed that a lot of good defence and, indeed, of good declarer play, is based on wishful thinking. Placing partner with the cards needed to defeat opponents' contract, or placing opponents' kings and queens in the right places when playing a contract, will lead to positive results surprisingly often.

Good Luck and Keep Calm

T his little book has given you the minimum of knowledge about the bidding and play of Contract Bridge. Now it's up to you to get your feet wet.

Your first few sessions at the Bridge table might give you mild jitters. You may stumble over things that experienced players take for granted and in their stride. This is all perfectly natural, normal and to be expected. You are a beginner. Don't be ashamed of it. Even the beetle-browed experts who glare at you over their cards were beginners once. Don't let them bully you. Charm them with your innocent eagerness to share their knowledge. After a hand is over, ask them how they would have bid it or played it. You'll learn something and you'll also pull their fangs.

Your worst jitters will come from occasional agonies of indecision. If you sit there stewing too long, you will irritate yourself and your opponents. It's much better to make the wrong bid or play after a reasonable pause. You can then apologise sweetly to your partner after he bites your head off as he explains why your bid or play was wrong. Again, you'll learn something.

Almost everybody loves a beginner. Your presence makes them feel smug and superior. The only really unpopular beginner is the one who makes the same mistakes over and over again.

Keep track of your goofs, either in your head or on a slip of paper. Then do something about them. Reread the section in this book that concerns itself with the areas in which you erred or embark on a more stringent programme of self-improvement.

This book is a cram course to enable a beginner to sit down at the Bridge table with as few qualms as possible. Here are a few suggestions for a more extensive course:

- **Study the 'free' Bridge lessons in your daily newspaper.** For the price of a daily paper, you can get a Bridge lesson from famous Bridge experts.

- **Play as often as you can.** Experience is the best teacher in Bridge, and experience in actual play helps you determine what areas are weakest in your game. Find three likeminded friends and play regularly in each other's homes.

- **Read Bridge books.** Bookshops and libraries are stuffed with Bridge books. Play often, but if you want to improve, study, too.

- **Take Bridge lessons.** Many colleges of further education run courses. Contact your local authority for details. Alternatively, the English Bridge Union (see below) will be able to help you find a Bridge teacher.

- **Be a 'kibitzer'.** Watch at the table of experts. Keeping your eyes and ears open can be enormously instructive, but be warned: kibitzers should be seen and not heard. Talkative kibitzers have been known to have had their heads bitten off – at the ankles.

- **Try playing Duplicate Bridge.** Contact the English Bridge Union, Broadfields, Bicester Road, Aylesbury HP19 8AZ. Tel: 01296 317200. E-mail: postmaster@ebu.co.uk. Website: www.ebu.co.uk. This is the national organisation for Duplicate Bridge and they will be able to tell you about clubs in your area. Most clubs have special introductory events for players who are new to Duplicate.

- **Play online.** The English Bridge Union has its own playing site. Another good playing site is www.bridgebase.com. Go to the site, follow the instructions and just cut in and play. The standard is very variable. Don't worry, there will always be someone worse than you!

On this note, I wish you all the luck – and aces – in the world.

Index